AF428342

GEORGIA SWEETHEART

Who is Brittish to me and what future do I want for her?

From the time she was born, we knew she was destined to be a star. Brittish is very loving, creative, kind,
determined and so much more. She has always wanted to be someone others look up to. She believes in spreading kindness through her platform of "Beautiful Girls Like Me" This has been such a life impacting journey for her. She wants everyone to feel comfortable in their skin and to never question how beautiful they are. In response to this, she is coming out with a new book called Beautiful Girls Like Me Coming from a Small Town with Big Dreams. As her mom, I wish for Brittish to be whoever she desires to be, I wishful her to be the star she wants to be. She wants to be an inspiration for others and with support from family and friends, she will be.

What do you think about yourself?

I feel good about myself. I am loved, beautiful, sweet and a go getter.

What do you want to do in the future?

I want to be a makeup artist and continue my pageant career and be a *star*.

What is your favorite saying?

"I am Brave and I am Beautiful"

Beautiful girls like me can do anything they set their minds to do.

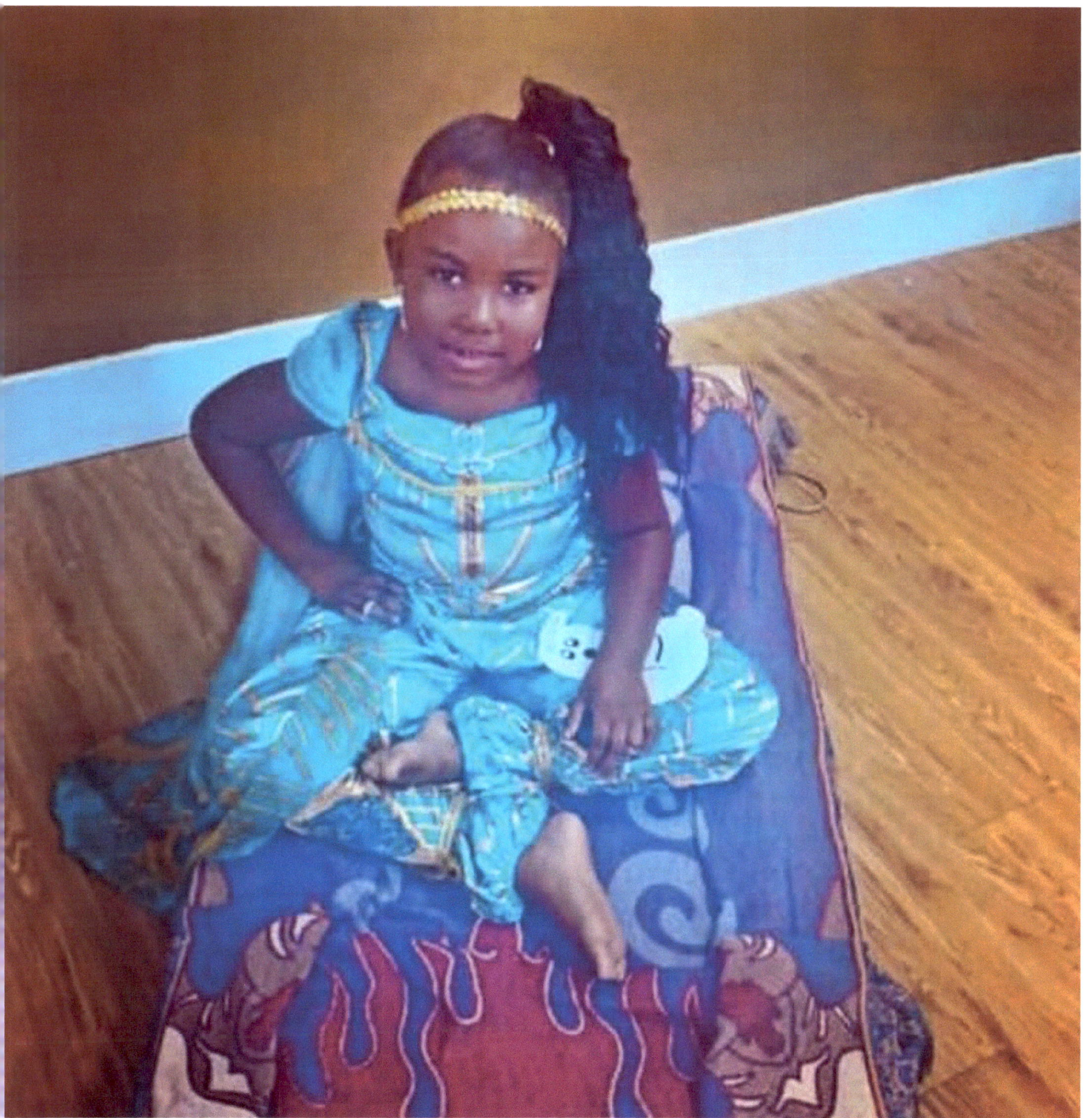

We are smart and we are blessed and we can do what we want to do.

Hello beautiful girls like me.
What do you see?

PERFORMANCE HALL
Lower

I see faces that are so beautiful. When you look in the mirror, be proud of what you see.

ool
9432

We are amazing and we are enough.

Trojans
WEE BALL

Nothing can *stop* a beautiful girl like me.

NEVER GIVE UP YOUR TIME
IS COMING ! THE RIGHT
CROWN WILL FIND YOU .

Even when life gets hard, just know that you matter and you are worthy.

Set your dreams high and don't let no one tell you that you cant be anything you want to be.

Beautiful girls like me we are unique and different and unlike anyone else.

Beautiful girls like me, we shine like no other. We are stars waiting for the perfect time to glow and show the world how beautiful we truly are.

"Girl, you are the creator
of your own reality."

MISS GEORGIA ELEMENT
TOO

"Being happy never goes out of style."

"Courageous girls are gorgeous."

TWIN OAKS
FUN FARM & MARKE
THANKFUL

"Confidence is the most beautiful thing a girl can wear."

"Beauty isn't about having a pretty face. It's about having a pretty mind, a pretty heart, and a pretty soul."

"A girl should be two things,
classy and fabulous."

GEORGIA ELEMENTARY

"Chin up, Princess."

"Girl, you are nothing less
than fireworks."

"The best color in the whole world is the one that looks good on you."

GEORGIA ELEM

"You are beautiful, capable, smart and worthy."